The Dad Dictionary

Written by:

Chris Brethwaite, Bill Bridgeman, Bill Gray, Allyson Jones, Kevin Kinzer, Mark Oatman, Scott Oppenheimer, Dan Taylor, Rich Warwick and Myra Zirkle.

Designed and Illustrated by:
Payton Kelly

 **ALGEBRA**: A form of math that Dad will offer to help you with, then puzzle over for 10 minutes, then tell you to reread the textbook.

AMATEUR: A dad who doesn't own a lawn spreader.

APPRECIATION: A prehistoric concept not taught in today's schools.

4

ARGUING: What Mom and Dad are <u>not</u> doing. They are having a "discussion."

ARTIFICIAL TURF: Plastic strands resembling grass which under Dad's care would die.

AUTO: A motor vehicle Dad owns in name only, and gains access to when in need of repair, fuel or cleaning.

BALANCE: The skill most often associated with making a snack, i.e., the ability to close a refrigerator door with one foot while holding its entire contents between your neck and shoulders.

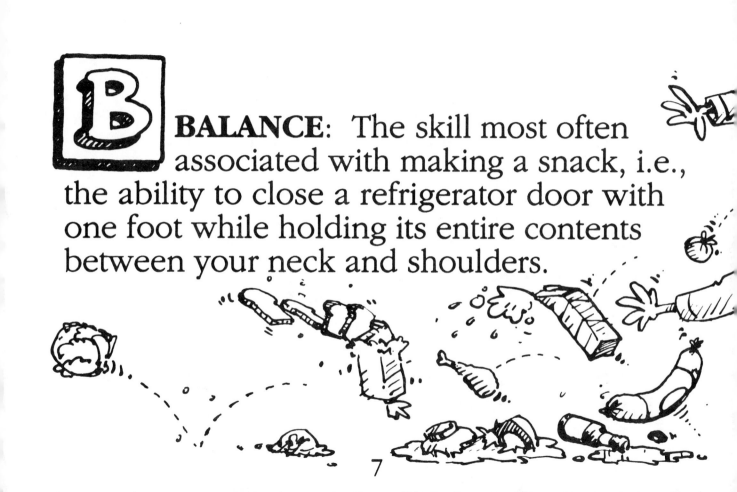

BASEBALL: A game played by a bunch of spoiled punks without half the natural ability Dad had when he was in school.

BASS: A delicious fresh water game fish that costs about $300 a serving when you figure in the cost of the bait, the tackle and the cost of retrieving the submerged car.

BATHROOM: A small room with a sink, tub and commode available to Dad for approximately five minutes per week.

BELCH: Something Dad tries to explain by saying they consider it a compliment in Japan.

失礼!!!

BOBBER: 1) A fishing accessory attached to the line. 2) A nickname for Dad's friend, Bob.

BOWLING: An indoor sport which offers Dad the opportunity to get some exercise, hang out with the guys and wear shoes even funnier looking than the ones he usually wears.

BOXER SHORTS: A type of underpants that are actually larger than the pants they are under. Preferred by dads everywhere.

A.

B.

BROTHER-IN-LAW: A guy without a job, or a guy with a job he will soon lose. Just hope and pray he doesn't move in!

BRUNCH: Something that inspires Dad to say, "We don't say 'Lupper' for between lunch and supper, so why say 'Brunch'?" Then he chuckles to himself.

BUFFET: See "HEAVEN "

BUM: See: "DAUGHTER'S
BOYFRIEND "

CAMERA: A device used by Dad to remove the heads from family members.

CHAMP: What a boxer would be if he could only hear the instructions Dad was shouting from the couch.

CHARCOAL LIGHTER: 1) A type of fuel used to ignite charcoal. 2) What a real steak should taste like.

CHARGE CARDS: In Dad's eyes, little plastic keys to Debtor's Prison.

CLASH: The little war-in-progress on Dad's body.

CUSSING: See "GOLF," "UTILITY BILLS" or "HAND TOOLS "

 **DAD**: A male parent. From the Latin phrase "Daddus Shinglus Impactus" meaning "One who hits the roof."

DEAR: A term used by Mom on Dad in front of the kids, which, loosely translated, means "You're in big trouble now, Mister."

DELIVERY ROOM: A small room used by Dad to make home movies.

DENT: A small depression in Dad's car, which leads to a massive repair bill and the denial of responsibility by everyone in the family of driving age.

DOG: A remote control for the newspaper.

DOGS: Dad's clever nickname for feet, usually found in the phrase "My dogs are killin' me," after which Dad removes his shoes in an attempt to kill everyone else, too.

DRIVEWAY: A storage place for bikes, skateboards and other assorted toys.

EARLY BIRD: Worm-catching hero in one of Dad's lectures that applies to nothing and ends with yet another re-telling of how hard he worked on his paper route.

EARRING: Something a teenage son wears over Dad's dead body.

EAT: Function best performed in front of a blaring television.

ECSTASY: See "SUPER BOWL™"

FAMILY: A group of people whose job is to give Dad plenty of reasons to roll his eyes toward the ceiling and mumble "Give me strength!"

FAUCET: A device for channeling water, which drips until Dad fixes it. Then it leaks a steady stream.

FOUR-CYLINDER CAR: A blight on mankind. See "ARMAGEDDON"

FUNNY: What Dad thinks he's being when he says things like, "Workin' hard or hardly workin'?"

 **GARDEN OF EDEN**: A backyard with a hammock.

GARDENING: The act of growing food for mealybugs and rabbits.

GAS GUZZLER: See "NOW THAT'S A CAR!"

GOLF: A sport in which a small white ball is cussed at until it falls into a hole.

GOO GOO: A phrase spoken by dads to babies, which, roughly translated, means "Please don't spit up until your mother gets home."

"GRACE!": What Dad yells out when Mom asks if someone will say grace.

HAGGLE: What Dad does with used car dealers, thereby raising the cost of the car several hundred dollars.

HAIRCUT: A grooming procedure that gives Dads and their teenagers something to talk about at dinner.

HALF-BAKED: 1) An idea suggested by Dad's supervisor at work. 2) Anything baked by Dad.

HALIBUT: Why Dad says he fishes.

HARDWARE STORE: A Dad version of the Smithsonian.

HAT: An article of clothing worn by Dad because it looks good, and NOT to cover any bald spot, because there isn't any bald spot, and don't you forget it!

HUNTING: A sport on which Dad will spend hundreds of dollars for guns, clothing, licenses, etc., in order to provide the family with a couple of pounds of meat which no one will eat.

**IDIOT**: Dad's boss.

INCINERATE: See: "BARBECUE GRILL"

INFERIOR: Anything made overseas.

JERKY: A tough, dried-out food that is typically made by putting Dad in charge of scrambled eggs.

JOBLESS: See: "BROTHER-IN-LAW"

JUNK: Any automobile not equipped with cruise control.

 **KETCHUP**: Wonder nectar of the gods. The perfect accompaniment to any food.

KIDS: Small people who Dad feeds, clothes and supports. In return for this he annually receives a tie.

 **LAUGH**: Something Dad, and only Dad, does at his own jokes.

LECTURE: Dad's favorite mode of communication, usually prefaced by "When I was your age," "In my day," or "Kids these days."

LEND: In Dad's world, to give money with no prospect of seeing it again.

LIGHT SWITCH: A money ticker that has absolutely no business being turned on, unless you plan on being in the room for more than half an hour.

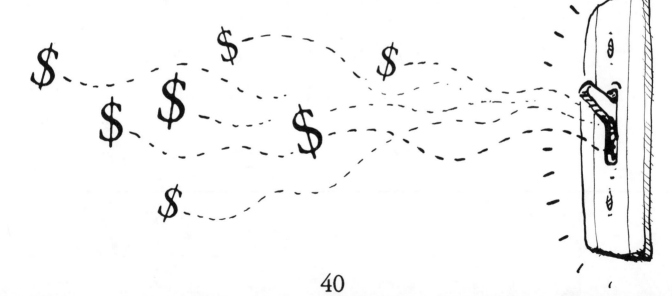

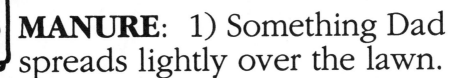**MANURE**: 1) Something Dad spreads lightly over the lawn. 2) Something Dad spreads heavily over a fishing story.

MAYBE: A word used by dads when they mean "No."

MONEY: Something Dad is not made of. (Note: It doesn't grow on trees, either.)

MUD: The name of the kid who was messing with Dad's tools.

NAIL: A pointed metal object that Dad holds while striking his thumb with a hammer.

NAP: Something Dad is accused of doing when he's "resting his eyes."

NEIGHBOR: Dad's rival in the never-ending battle for supremacy in lawn beauty, barbecuing technique and car maintenance.

NEWSPAPER: Dad's blanket.

OLD FOOTBALL INJURY: An intermittent ache or pain, real or imagined, which prevents Dad from performing simple household chores.

ORTHODONTIST: The reason Dad doesn't own a vacation home.

OUTDOORS: The vast area that Dad's kids are constantly trying to heat.

PAGEANT: An event wherein Dad takes time off from work to see offspring portray historical figures, trees or vegetables.

PEACE AND QUIET: A state of being which dads constantly, endlessly yearn for, but never seem to reach.

PEEP: Dad had better not hear one. (Especially if he's "had enough.")

PEE WEE BASEBALL: A game played with a bat and ball on a field, between two teams of kids who pick clover and chase bees.

49

PIG OUT: To look upon all household foodstuffs as a personal gluttony challenge. Often done in conjunction with televised sports.

PLAID: The noisy intersection of contrasting perpendicular lines, preferably on a polyester format.

"POINTS," "PLUGS," "CONDENSER": Three words Dad drops into any and all automotive conversations in the false hope that he'll appear knowledgeable.

POWER RAKING: The one outdoor activity Dad would like to see become a professional sporting event.

PRETZELS: Dad's hors d'oeuvres.

**QUICHE**: You've gotta be kidding.

 **REFRIGERATOR**: Dad's second favorite appliance, right after the television.

REPAIR: See: "YELLOW PAGES"

RIDING MOWER: The closest Dad will ever come to owning a convertible.

ROAD MAP: A diagram of streets that can only be properly folded by a dad.

Ⓐ UNFOLDED   Ⓑ FOLDED

ROCK VIDEOS: An obvious Communist plot which will no doubt destroy the American way of life.

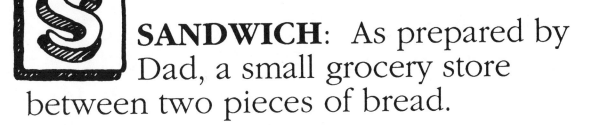 **SANDWICH**: As prepared by Dad, a small grocery store between two pieces of bread.

SIN: Using a straight claw hammer when a ball peen hammer is clearly the more appropriate tool.

"SLOW DOWN!": The first words out of Dad's mouth when teaching a kid to drive, usually followed by the mental notes, " We're gonna DIE!" and "I will never do this again. This is a job for Mom."

"SOME PEOPLE HAVE ALL THE LUCK": Dad's way of referring to anyone who experiences luck. He himself has never had luck.

STOP: Something kids had better do before Dad turns this thing around, and he means it!

SKRREEEEEE!!!

TACKLE BOX: A box used to hold Dad's fishing equipment, such as bottle opener, can opener, pocket radio, batteries, thermos, cream and sugar packs, matches, and, if room allows, a few hooks and bobbers.

TALK BACK: What kids won't do if they know what's good for them.

TURN SIGNALS: What wimps use.

UMPTEEN: The number of times Dad has to tell kids anything before they'll listen.

UNFINISHED: Any do-it-yourself project that Dad started.

UTOPIA: A bathroom with a magazine rack.

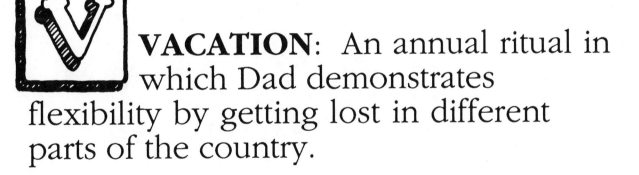 **VACATION**: An annual ritual in which Dad demonstrates flexibility by getting lost in different parts of the country.

VCR: A device which Dad tries to preset to record late-night movies, but winds up with two hours of the Weather Channel instead.

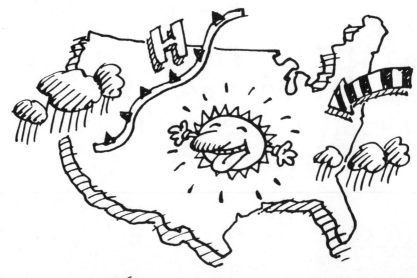

VOLTAGE: A word Dad bandies about just before sticking a screwdriver in a light socket and shorting out the house.

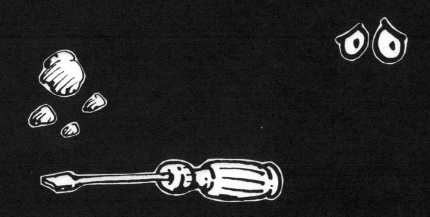

WALK: What Dad always did to school farther than anyone else, through deeper snow, up more hills, in flimsier shoes, with a greater sense of gratitude.

WEATHER: No reason to turn up the thermostat. It's fine where it is.

WEED AND FEED: 1) A lawn product containing a combination of weed killer and fertilizer. 2) The two-step process Dad uses when removing weeds. For example, pull a weed, eat a sandwich...pull a weed, eat some chips...pull a weed, eat some pretzels.

WOODWORKING: Hobby of many creative dads who outfit a well-appointed "shop" where they spend hours listening to ball games on a beat-up radio.

...THREE-AND-TWO COUNT... AND, HERE'S THE PITCH...

X-RAY VISION: The only explanation for how Dad knows what's behind a kid's back, under his bed, or buried in his underwear drawer.

 **"YES, SIR"**: An extinct phrase, reportedly used in the past by children.

YOUNG MAN/YOUNG LADY: The proper way to address a kid who is getting the "Too-big-for-your-britches" lecture.

 **ZEALOT**: A dad who rotates the tires on his car every 5000 feet.

ZEBRA: A derisive term for a vision-impaired referee who makes a call against Dad's team.

ZERO: The probability of Dad buying a new Porsche for teenage family members.

ZOYSIA: The other green stuff Dad worries about.

Other books from
SHOEBOX GREETINGS
(A tiny little division of Hallmark)

HEY GUY, ARE YOU: A) Getting Older? B) Getting Better? C) Getting Balder?

FRISKY BUSINESS: All About Being Owned by a Cat.

THE WORLD ACCORDING TO DENISE.

GIRLS JUST WANNA HAVE FACE LIFTS: The Ugly Truth About Getting Older.

DON'T WORRY, BE CRABBY: Maxine's Guide to Life.

EVERYTHING YOU ALWAYS WANTED TO KNOW ABOUT STRESS...but were too nervous, tense, irritable and moody to ask.

40: THE YEAR OF NAPPING DANGEROUSLY.

RAIDERS OF THE LOST BARK: A Collection of Canine Cartoons.

THE MOM DICTIONARY.

WAKE UP AND SMELL THE FORMULA: The A to No ZZZZ's of Having a Baby.

WORKIN' NOON TO FIVE: The Official Workplace Quizbook.

THE OFFICIAL COLLEGE QUIZ BOOK.

WHAT...ME, 30?

STILL MARRIED AFTER ALL THESE YEARS.

YOU EXPECT ME TO SWALLOW THAT?: The Official Hospital Quiz Book.

THE GOOD, THE PLAID, AND THE BOGEY: A Glossary of Golfing Terms.

THE COLLEGE DICTIONARY: A Book You'll Actually Read!

THE FISHING DICTIONARY: Everything You'll Say About the One That Got Away.